MISSION:
TAX ZERO

MISSION: TAX ZERO

The Guide To Greatly Reduce Taxes In Retirement

JOSH BRADLEY

WEALTH AUTHORITY BOOKS

MISSION: TAX ZERO

The Guide To Greatly Reduce Taxes In Retirement

ISBN 13: 978-1-966168-24-9
ebook ISBN: 978-1-966168-25-6
Library of Congress Control Number: 2025910888

Designed by Melissa Farr, Back Porch Creative, LLC

WEALTH AUTHORITY BOOKS
2511 WOODLANDS WAY
OCEANSIDE, CA 92054
www.indiebooksintl.com

Wealth Authority Books is an imprint of Indie Books International®, Inc.

Contents

Foreword

When I first set out on my path to becoming a CPA, I envisioned myself not just as someone who prepared tax returns but as a trusted advisor who could help clients navigate the complexities of their finances and avoid costly missteps. In those early years, however, I found myself caught in the cycle of compliance work, focused on checking boxes and meeting deadlines. While tax returns are important, I soon realized that something was missing—a deeper connection with clients and a clearer understanding of their long-term financial goals.

The realization was humbling, and I was falling short. I was so focused on the technical side of tax preparation that I wasn't truly serving my clients in the way I had imagined.

This wasn't the impact I had hoped for when I first became a CPA. I knew I had to change.

I made the decision to step away from the narrow focus of compliance and embrace the broader role of a financial educator and guide. It became clear to me that tax returns were just the tip of the iceberg. My real job was to help my clients understand their financial landscape, how their decisions today could impact their future, how to avoid common pitfalls, and how to take advantage of opportunities they might not have known existed.

This book represents the culmination of that journey. It's not just about taxes or numbers—it's about helping you, the reader, understand the larger picture and make informed decisions that protect your financial well-being and your legacy. The goal is to arm you with the knowledge you need to navigate and avoid the mistakes that can lead to costly consequences, especially as you approach or are currently in retirement.

Retirement is a time for reflection, relaxation, and enjoying the fruits of a lifetime of hard work. However, for many, it also comes with a set of financial complexities—one of the most significant being taxes. While we often look forward to the day we can step away from the workforce, it's crucial to recognize that the choices we make today will impact our financial future tomorrow, including how much we will owe in taxes once we've stopped earning a regular paycheck.

Whether you're twenty years away, approaching retirement, or in retirement, this book will help you rethink how you approach your finances. I invite you to read this book not just as a technical guide but as a conversation about your future. Let's move beyond the numbers and embrace a strategy that empowers you to make better, more informed financial choices. With this knowledge in hand, you can step into retirement with confidence, knowing that you've taken the necessary steps to minimize tax liabilities and maximize your financial security.

Alli Dilloian Stephen, CPA

PREAMBLE

The Government's Budget Problem Is Your Retirement Tax Problem

The preamble of the United States Constitution is composed of a mere fifty-two words. It covers the basics as a way of introduction:

Who: "We the People"

What: "this Constitution of the United States of America"

Why: "in order to form a more perfect Union, establish Justice, insure domestic Tranquility, provide for the common defense, promote the general Welfare, and secure the Blessings of Liberty to ourselves and our Posterity."

Well, here we are well over two hundred years later, and all those important functions cost money. We can debate how wisely (or not) your tax dollars are spent, but whatever we think of them, the government certainly wants to collect them.

This book is a careful look at how, in retirement, you've already given plenty to Uncle Sam and how to keep your tax burden in retirement as close to zero as possible.

I grew up in the country in South Carolina. My dad worked at a factory making electrical boxes. He'd wake up at four in the morning, go to work, and come home. He was tired, too tired to go grocery shopping.

My mom was a teacher. After a long day with a classroom full of rowdy kids, she'd also be too tired to go grocery shopping. So, Mom would take us grocery shopping on the weekends. When you lived in the country, it was what city folks might call a "schlep" to Columbia or Sumter, the nearest towns. It was the better part of an hour round trip anytime you went to the grocery store.

The ideal situation for my mom was to only make that trip every other weekend. So, every other weekend, she'd get me and my sister in the car. We would make that long drive to the grocery store. Then she'd spend three hours in this grocery store. I might be exaggerating a little. Maybe it was only two and a half hours, but the entire experience was at least three hours every other weekend. Miserable.

Not one for any messing around, Mom told us we could have one food request. There was no whining for items that caught our eye in every aisle. One request, and we knew not to ask for more.

We had to take turns picking, but she always let one of us pick out the cereal. My sister, who was older than me, stronger than me, and smarter than me, would spend the first two hours abusing me to try to get me out of my pick. Many times, I am sad to say she succeeded. But sometimes, I'd stand firm and get my pick of cereal. I loved all the sugary cereals—Lucky Charms, Cinnamon Toast Crunch, Cocoa Pebbles—to name just a few. But I was a smart kid. I knew back in the late eighties and early nineties that omega-3 fatty acids were critical for heart and health development, and my favorite cereal was Honey Bunches of Oats with almonds because that's where you get the omega-3s.

I'd say, "Mom, I want the Honey Bunches of Oats."

She'd say, "Josh, you're so smart. Science will catch up to you in ten years. Omega-3s are important. That's my favorite cereal, too."

Awesome! A wish granted!

But then, sometimes, she would say, "But I need you to reach below the Bunches of Oats."

What's below the Bunches of Oats, you ask? It's the store brand that may as well have been called Bucket of Oats.

"Mom, Bucket of Oats? They don't even have real almonds in that. They take cardboard; they press it together, and they paint it. There are no omega-3 fatty acids in cardboard."

To this day, I smile as I ask my mom, "Was the five cents you saved worth the health and development of your children?"

She will not answer that. But you know what she buys for the grandkids? Honey Bunches of Oats! Then she'll buy an extra bag of almond slivers and add them to give her grandbabies an extra protein boost and those omega-3s. She understands the economics of grandparenthood.

When Mom orchestrated my sister and me through our biweekly grocery trip, she didn't care. She'd make me get the Bucket of Oats with honey and almond substitute.

Why did she make me get the Bucket of Oats? I say this with love, but she was cheap. Cheap's the word. She was cheap. Now, having learned from the best, I'm cheap, too. I follow that desire to save with everything I do.

However, what I learned from those trips to the grocery store is that saving a nickel on cereal is not always the smart thing to do. There is more to financial acumen than saving your pennies here and there.

I want to find every penny I can for people, so what's wrong with being cheap? I'm here to tell you that we've been taught to be cheap, cheap, cheap when it comes to taxes. To have the kind of life we want now and well into retirement, there is more to the equation than saving pennies here and there. I want you to thrive in retirement, not just survive. I want people to get the value of those Honey Bunches of Oats with real almonds. Nobody wants the Bucket of Oats with honey and almond substitute.

To get to that "Honey Bunches of Oats" kind of life, I am here to:

1. Sound the alarm if you are over fifty so you understand what is at stake.
2. Help you understand how tax laws impact your retirement income and tax liability.
3. Help you be aware of all the areas in which taxation can impact retirees and how to control them where we can:
    a. Federal income tax
    b. State income tax
    c. Social Security
    d. Medicare
    e. Capital gains
    f. Estate tax
    g. Net Investment Income Tax

4. Reset your mindset: We have been trained to be cheap; we need to focus on paying the least in a lifetime.

What's My Motivation?

How did I get so concerned about helping people make the most of their retirement years, starting with their tax burden? That nasty box of Buckets of Oats, for starters.

Beyond that, I saw what was happening in my industry and a need to address the elephant in the room.

For the longest time, my firm helped people prepare for retirement in the standard ways: through 401(k)s and IRAs, investments, CDs, life insurance—all the usual tactics. Then, in 2018, the Tax Cut and Jobs Act was passed. I did a deep dive to study the possible implications for my clients.

I realized that in 2026, our clients—along with many other Americans—would be paying more taxes. In 2020, we took steps to get ahead of this, bringing a tax firm and several CPAs under the umbrella of our company. We wanted to get this information out to our clients and as many other people as possible.

By taking steps to protect assets and manage tax liabilities, we've found the average tax savings will be over $100,000 for these families versus people who follow the old rules for retirement accounts. By launching Mission Tax Zero and writing this book, my whole team and I are on a mission to have people pay as little taxes in retirement as possible.

The Power Of Zero

The Power of Zero by David McKnight[1] is a popular book, used widely in the financial planning industry. I wanted to, well, zero in on an area McKnight covers: getting as close to zero tax in retirement as possible.

How do you approach zero taxes in retirement? Just as importantly, is it even worth it?

Taxes don't tend to go down over time, so the goal of *Mission: Tax Zero* is to help you find every way you can to get at or close to zero tax liability in retirement. Wouldn't that be awesome?

You've probably been socking money away in IRAs and 401(k)s for years. We love that tax-deferred goodness, but the bill is coming due sooner than you think. Because taxes tend to go up over time, later money for the government is worth more than if they tax you on that money today. Let me say that another way: The tax rate for that deferred money will likely be higher than what you are being taxed today. That's the bargain we make with those savings instruments.

I want to help you look beyond these basic tools to the reality of what you will face regarding tax burdens in your retirement years. Let's eliminate as much of that burden as possible with the goal of getting you to *Tax Zero*.

Training Your Tax Mindset

My mom was a teacher, and for a hot minute, I tried out teaching, too. I am a big believer in education. When it comes to finances, I thought that if I got smarter about taxes and investments, I'd make good decisions. What I realized is that, yes, education matters. However, the biggest reason we make bad financial decisions has nothing to do with education.

Educate yourself, absolutely, but understand the role that emotions play in how you spend and save. Emotions are a massive factor in financial decisions, no matter what level of financial literacy we achieve. That's why we need to talk about mindset before diving into tax-saving strategies.

The mindset we've been trained to have is deferral. We don't have to worry about taxes on our retirement savings, because they are being deferred! Sweet, fancy Moses, we don't ever have to think about taxes on those IRAs and 401(k)s, right?

Wrong.

So, putting those deferred taxes out of sight and out of mind is the first mistake. Then we are told that in retirement, we'll be on a "fixed income." Somehow, we have come to believe that fixed income = lower tax bracket. Is that true?

In Tax-Zero terms, your 401(k) is not for you alone. It's for you and the government. They are more than happy to see you put money away there. You put in five grand a year, and they give you a tax deduction. That sounds like a win-win, but is it?

Let's say you build up a nest egg in your retirement accounts of at least one million dollars. Then throughout your lifetime and that of your heirs, you're paying taxes on over a million dollars. The IRS gave you a small deduction over the years that you contributed to the 401(k). When the dollars have accumulated and tax rates have certainly not gone down, they turn around and collect hundreds of thousands of dollars. The government wins in this scenario, but where does that leave you? To change this status quo, you've got to change your mindset.

Finding Your Way Out Of The Deferment Matrix

The challenge in changing your mindset is that you now need to take a more active role in managing your retirement income and tax burden. The government is happy to take on that burden of thinking for you, but there is a price to pay for that mental "deferment."

We've been trained—downright indoctrinated—to never, ever, under any circumstances, give the government one penny of taxes before they come and rip it out of our hands.

At this point in discussions with clients, I feel like Morpheus explaining the Matrix to Neo. "What if I told you the interest you defer now will be worth less than the interest you pay later?" Like Neo's journey out of the Matrix, it might take you some time to come to terms with this acknowledgment of reality that we've been hiding from ourselves for so long.

It was hidden away from me for many years. Here is how my eyes were opened.

My favorite investment method is a certificate of deposit (CD) because it is a safe place to store money and get a decent rate of return. I thought that if I could make people more interested in their CDs, it would solve all their problems.

My grandmother came to me one day—naturally, I was her favorite—to ask for my help with her and Grandpa's retirement money. They were making it work with two social security checks plus a little nest egg to protect from the what-ifs.

I asked her, "What do you have it in?"

She said it was in the bank in CDs.

I said, "Well, that's perfect. I'm a CD salesman. What interest rate are you making?"

At that time, in the early 2000s, it was making 3 percent. I got her a 6-percent FDIC-insured CD. I doubled her return, guaranteed. Grandma and Grandpa were one of my first clients. I felt like the king of the world. I was solving all the world's problems. We were only a couple of years from world peace, out there, earning interest for my grandparents and my other clients.

I thought everything was just fine. We renewed their CDs several times over the next few years, all at amazing rates, until about three years later when she came to me with a big problem.

My grandfather had passed away, which meant she was now living on one Social Security check. You don't get both spouses' benefits when one passes away; you get the higher of the two. But even so, this was enough to pay her bills.

Meanwhile, the CD I invested in for her had grown to over $100,000. That's 50 percent more than what she had.

Grandma came to me because she was about to go into long-term care, and she was afraid that she would lose their financial legacy on her watch. She was scared to death and stressed out.

The Capital Confidence Plan

I thought CD interest was the ultimate fix. I thought the rate of return was all that mattered. In these conversations with my grandmother, I realized that investments matter, but many other factors matter even more. That's how we created our Capital Confidence Plan[2] and identified five areas that have the biggest impact on successful retirement to get you through with as much fun, purpose, and financial security as possible.

I never want to see somebody go through that again. Over the next eighteen months, her $100,000 went down to nothing, and she was stressed. Every month I was stressed, feeling like I'd failed to address that. I could have made her 20 percent on her CD, but she still would have lost it all.

That experience started a relentless pursuit of what really matters in managing retirement income, savings, and investments. She wouldn't have been in that position if I'd found these solutions earlier. It's all about a good income plan, taxes, investments, healthcare, and estate plans. And so that's how we created our Capital Confidence Plan.

The plan addresses the top five areas with the biggest impact of making it through retirement with as much joy as possible while maintaining your financial dignity. Here are the steps:

1. **Income Plan:** Do you know how much you need each month after taxes and adjusted for inflation? Do you know how to turn all those assets you accumulated—Social Security, pensions, 401(k)s, real estate—into cash flow that will last the rest of your life? Everyone should have a detailed income plan to show whether they can accomplish their goals and not run out.

2. **Investments:** Investment rules while in the workforce are straightforward: Invest early and often and get a good rate of return. You can expect some down

years, and your investment strategy should account for those. In retirement, the rules change a little. The rate of return matters, but those down years can be catastrophic. When you need to pull funds out to fund your retirement, down years can force you to sell investments at a permanent loss.

Everyone needs to have an investment plan to provide at least the next five years' worth of income without the risk of downturns in the market. Emotions can lead to bad financial decisions. Watching account values go down can be hard to stomach, but in retirement, those same drops can cause us to make emotional decisions about our investments. Everyone needs to understand the risk they are willing to stick with and make sure their investments are in line.

3. **Taxes:** We all need to have a plan to address tax liabilities, which is why we wrote this book.

4. **Health Care:** For most retirees, taxes and health-related expenses are the biggest costs. Long-term care is usually the top reason retirees go broke. Everyone should have a plan to address their Medicare coverage and address their risk for long-term care expenses.

5. **Legacy:** When you pass away, you want your assets to move as quickly as possible to your loved ones and the causes you care about, with the government

getting as little as possible. You also want to ensure that you have documents—like health care directives and power of attorney—in place to help care for you while you are still living.

The **Capital Confidence Plan** helps people develop a tax mindset that looks beyond deferred taxes and rates of return to build the resources that will carry them through their retirement years.

What will the government do with tax laws? That's anybody's guess, but a dramatic reduction in tax burden is not how the government rolls.

With that in mind, through the following pages, I want to walk you through the best strategies I have found to keep the government out of your pockets during retirement.

Eight Great Tax-Zero Strategy Steps:

1. **Shift Your Tax Allocation:** A common saying goes, "The easiest way to guarantee a higher rate of return on investments is not what you own but where you own it." My take on that concept: The easiest way to make more money is to pay less taxes.

2. **Harvest Your Tax Losses:** Sell investments that have lost money and claim them on your tax return.

3. **Take Advantage Of Permanent Life Insurance:** A whole life insurance policy is your money. It's like

being your own bank. Borrow from the cash value and leverage your money. Permanent life can provide multiple ways to access funds tax-free.

4. **Control Taxes With Annuities:** Learn why 80 percent of annuities are wrong for 80 percent of potential purchasers.

5. **Give Wisely To Charity:** Since the Tax Act of 2018, charitable giving is no longer automatically deductible. I'll share three strategies for giving wisely.

6. **Save With A Healthcare Spending Account:** I call this the holy grail of Tax Zero. This is deductible spending, but you've got to use it to get the advantage.

7. **Convert To A Roth IRA:** Why Roth? Because taxes go up, not down.

8. **Utilize Tax-Free (Sort Of) Bonds:** This is one of the simplest Tax-Zero strategies, with some important caveats.

I have seen how these strategies help people build a life in retirement that keeps Uncle Sam from taking a bigger bite than he is due. What I want you to gain from the following pages is that Mission: Tax Zero, should you choose to accept it, is within your reach.

CHAPTER ONE

Why You Need To Think Now About Tax-Zero Retirement

I'm cheap. I was raised cheap. Every penny matters. That is why I love to help people manage the pennies and dollars to live as stress-free as possible in their retirement years. You have a plan for retirement of sorts—with the IRAs and 401(k)s—but who is this Tax-Zero stuff for? Are you too late or too early to start planning this way?

Let's start with a fable. Once, there were two grasshoppers. The first grasshopper saved and saved, and the other fiddled a lot and didn't save as much but had a great advisor who used diversified strategies to build wealth and minimize tax liability. Who knew grasshopper society was so complex?

Anyway, the first grasshopper who saved ended up with less money in retirement than the one who didn't save as much but had better tax strategies.

The moral: saving is great, but it is only the first step. It's really the step before the first step. To build wealth and keep more of it for yourself in retirement, you need a Tax-Zero strategy that is even better than the second grasshopper. I mean, how big can a grasshopper's retirement plan possibly be?

The Myth Of Lower Expenses In Retirement

You've bought and sold a house or two and spent money to raise your kids and get them established in the world. Now, the major expenses in life are in the rearview mirror, right?

The reality is something much different. Many people I work with end up spending more in retirement. Two key ingredients are responsible for this reality. You've got more time and often fewer fixed expenses. But you've also got a bucket list of things you want to do. You want to enjoy life. You want to travel, see the grandkids, spend money on the grandkids, and buy them name-brand cereal with almonds.

This book is not for the super-rich. They find loopholes and have plenty left over after paying taxes. This book is for those who work hard, save and sock money away, and have to keep an eye on it. You've found your way through personal and global economic ups and downs and lived to tell the tale. You want what you have built to last through these years and hopefully have some left to pass on to the kids and grandkids. If that sounds like you, I have found that this is exactly the demographic for whom taxes can become a burden in retirement. It doesn't have to be that way.

Am I Too Late For Zero Tax?

The good news is, whoever you are in the not-super-rich camp, you are not too late to start these eight Tax-Zero strategies.

Sometimes, people are concerned that though they're in their high-earning years now, they're in a higher bracket, but when they're retired, they'll be living on less money, so they're in a lower bracket. That is a common misconception.

In retirement, you also lose a lot of deductions. You usually don't have your kids to deduct. Hopefully, your mortgage has been paid down to a small amount or nothing at all. With all of this work done, a lot of your ability to deduct goes down. In retirement, you are less likely to be actively saving, at least not like you did in your forties and fifties.

Here's one way to look at the situation. I might make $100,000 when I'm earning, but if I'm putting ten grand away into my 401(k), how much am I making? Ninety thousand. The good news is, if you have $90,000 of income in retirement, you're actually netting the same as when you were making six figures.

Without these strategies, you might be making less in retirement, but what you're spending and paying taxes on stays the same. Then, as you lose deductions, you could be in a higher tax bracket in retirement. When the tax brackets reset in 2026, if your bracket was 22 percent, that turns into 25 percent. That's heading in the wrong direction, so finding ways to mitigate the effects of heading into a different tax bracket is important.

The point is that you can start using some of these strategies while you are still earning to make your retirement taxes as close to zero as possible.

Have A Plan

Before you go rushing into these strategies, there is a crucial step to take. You can't do a true tax plan without having an income plan. How much will you need each month, each year, in retirement? Reality check: if you've saved nothing, you'll live on nothing, and tax planning is kind of a waste of time for you.

Understanding longevity is something many of us are reluctant to think about, yet it is a necessary part of retirement planning. In a 2023 *Fast Company* article,[3] author Emily Guy Birken writes, "Weak longevity literacy can lead to insufficient retirement income in one of two ways: Either you are simply not thinking about death (because who wants to?) or you are underestimating how long you will live."

That's why the first step of tax planning isn't the tax portion. It's having an income plan, so you know how much you need and how to realistically get to that goal. So, you need to know your income today and then in the future to do a real tax plan.

Once your income plan is in place, you can start your Mission: Tax Zero plan. You must have two pieces of knowledge to do a real tax plan: where you stand today and then where you'll be in ten years. None of us knows exactly what will happen in ten years, but you need to have a solid idea based on your recent past and a reasonable estimation of the future to start a zero-tax plan.

Now comes the fun part: putting the pieces of your tax plan together with these eight tested zero-tax strategies.

CHAPTER 2

One Plus One Equals...?

Growing up in the country, a trip into town was always a long haul. My mom, being a teacher, would make these interminable rides even worse by peppering me and my sister with math questions. Now, I look back on what I thought of as torment with a great deal of fondness. As a result of those quizzes, from an early age, I became very good at math. To this day I can probably win a math challenge, as long as we're competing at a fifth-grade level.

Not everyone has the benefit of compulsory math tutoring. But most of us know that one plus one equals two. That's how normal math works. But when it comes to taxes in retirement, one plus one does not equal two. When it comes to taxes, because of the many well-intentioned things we were taught to do prior to retirement, the equation can get out of whack. These practices can leave you with a tax bill exponentially larger than one plus one equaling two.

What do I mean by that? Many people, when they retire, are in the 12 percent tax bracket. You may be thinking, "Josh, that sounds pretty good. I'd love to pay no taxes, but 12 percent is not that bad. Why do I need to care about taxes?" The problem will come in your early to mid-seventies. Currently, required minimum distributions (RMDs) kick in at age seventy-three to seventy-five. You'll be required to make withdrawals from qualified accounts, like IRAs and your 401(k).

2025 Tax Highlights

Ordinary Income & Short-Term Capital Gains

Tax Brackets (Single)				Tax Brackets (Joint)			
Tax Rate	2017	Tax Rate	2025	Tax Rate	2017	Tax Rate	2025
10%	$9,325 or less	10%	$11,925 or less	10%	$18,650 or less	10%	$23,850 or less
15%	$9,326-$37,950	12%	$11,925-$48,475	15%	$18,651-$75,900	12%	$23,850-$96,950
25%	$37,951-$91,900	22%	$48,475-$103,350	25%	$75,901-$153,100	22%	$96,950-$206,700
28%	$91,901-$191,650	24%	$103,350-$197,300	28%	$153,101-$233,550	24%	$206,700-$394,600
33%	$191,651-$416,701	32%	$197,300-$250,525	33%	$233,351-$416,700	32%	$394,600-$501,050
35%	$416,701-$418,400	35%	$250,525-$626,350	35%	$416,701-$470,700	35%	$501,050-$751,600
39.60%	Over $418,400	37%	Over $626,350	39.60%	Over $470,700	37%	Over $751,600

Long-Term Capital Gains

Tax Rate	2017	2025	Tax Rate	2017	2025
0%	$37,950 or less	$48,350 or less	0%	$75,900 or less	$96,700 or less
15%	$37,951-$418,400	$48,350-$533,400	15%	$75,901-$470,700	$96,700-$600,050
20%	Over $418,400	Over $533,400	20%	Over $470,700	Over $600,050

Dividends Estate and Gifts

Ordinary Dividends (2017-2025)	Taxed at ordinary income rates	Estate Tax Exemption (2025): $13.99 Million per person; $27.98 Million per couple with a 40% top tax rate
Qualifying Dividends (2017-2025)	Taxed at long-term capital gains rates	Exemption Amount (2017): $5.9 million per person; $10.98 million per couple with a 40% tax rate
		Annual gift exclusion (2025): $19,000 per donor, to each recipient

Net Investment Income Tax	Additional Medicare Tax
3.8% surtax on net investment income with modified adjusted gross income above $200,000 (single) and $250,000 (joint).	Income above $200,000 (single) and $250,000 (joint) is taxed an additional 0.9%.

Standard Deduction *

	Single	Joint
2017	$6,350	$12,700
2025	$15,000	$30,000

*For individuals over the age of 65 or blind, an additional $1,600 per person for married filers and $2,000 for single of Head of Household filers.

Created by Capital City Financial Partners from information found at https://www.irs.gov/newsroom/irs-releases-tax-inflation-adjustments-for-tax-year-2025

Taking this money out of those accounts might tip you from the 12 percent tax bracket to the 25 percent tax bracket. With your tax bracket more than doubled, that's one plus one equals three or four. But that's not the end of the problem. That RMD can cause higher Medicare taxes based on your RMD-bloated income. With increased Medicare premiums—about $2,000 to $3,000 more a year—you've gone from one plus one equals two to one plus one equals six or seven.

Medicare Part B

Medicare 2025 Part B Premiums by Income If your filing status and yearly income in 2023 was:			(In 2025) Each month you pay
File Individual Tax Return	File Joint Tax Return	File Married & Separate Tax Return	
$106k or less	$212k or less	$106k or less	$185.00
Above $106k up to $133k	Above $212k up to $266k	N/A	$259.00
Above $133k up to $167k	Above $266k up to $334k	N/A	$370.00
Above $167k up to $200k	Above $334k up to $400k	N/A	$480.90
Above $200k & less than $500k	Above $400k & less than $750k	Above $106k & less than $394k	$591.90
$500k or above	$750k and above	$394k and above	$628.90

Medicare Part D

Medicare 2025 Part D Premiums by Income If your filing status and yearly income in 2023 was:			(In 2025) Each month you pay
File Individual Tax Return	File Joint Tax Return	File Married & Separate Tax Return	
$106k or less	$212k or less	$106k or less	Your plan premium
Above $106k up to $133k	Above $212k up to $266k	N/A	$13.70 + your plan premium
Above $133k up to $167k	Above $266k up to $334k	N/A	$35.30 + your plan premium
Above $167k up to $200k	Above $334k up to $400k	N/A	$57.00 + your plan premium
Above $200k & less than $500k	Above $400k & less than $750k	Above $106k & less than $394k	$78.60 + your plan premium
$500k or above	$750k and above	$394k and above	$85.80 + your plan premium

Created by Capital City Financial Partners from information found at https://www.medicare.gov/publications/11579-medicare-costs.pdf

But wait, there's more. Then, you have to worry about Social Security taxes. Social Security taxes are based on a whole different formula, not the same as your Medicare brackets or your tax brackets. It can make you go from 0 percent taxable to 85 percent taxable. Then we worry about capital gains rates that can increase with these forced distributions as well as net investment taxes and many more.

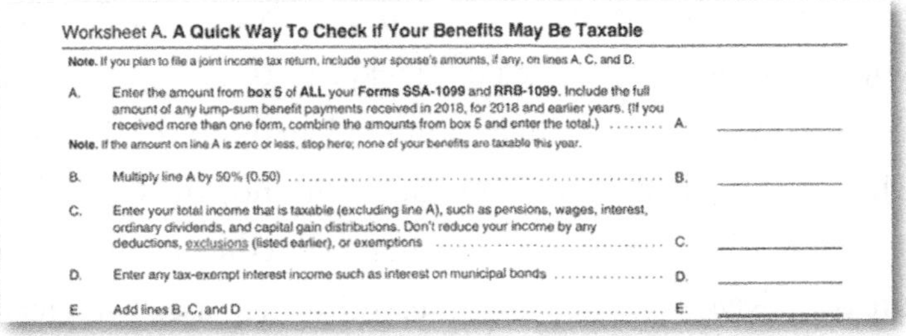

Worksheet A. **A Quick Way To Check if Your Benefits May Be Taxable**

Note. If you plan to file a joint income tax return, include your spouse's amounts, if any, on lines A, C, and D.

A.	Enter the amount from **box 5** of **ALL** your **Forms SSA-1099** and **RRB-1099.** Include the full amount of any lump-sum benefit payments received in 2018, for 2018 and earlier years. (If you received more than one form, combine the amounts from box 5 and enter the total.)	A.	
Note.	If the amount on line A is zero or less, stop here; none of your benefits are taxable this year.		
B.	Multiply line A by 50% (0.50)	B.	
C.	Enter your total income that is taxable (excluding line A), such as pensions, wages, interest, ordinary dividends, and capital gain distributions. Don't reduce your income by any deductions, exclusions (listed earlier), or exemptions	C.	
D.	Enter any tax-exempt interest income such as interest on municipal bonds	D.	
E.	Add lines B, C, and D	E.	

https://www.irs.gov/pub/irs-pdf/p915.pdf page 4

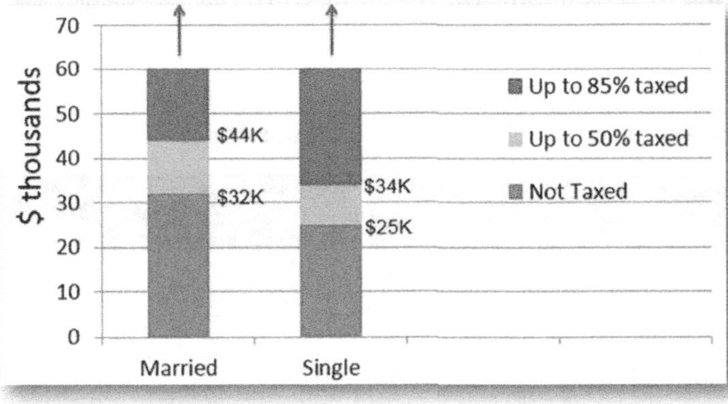

Created by Capital City Financial Partners

When it comes to retirement taxes, that same old formula of one plus one equals two is not accurate. It's really one plus one, which maybe equals nine, ten, or eleven. That is why it is so important for people heading into retirement to have a crystal-clear view and plan around taxes. It's not as simple as looking at your likely tax bracket in those first years of retirement.

I help clients every day to see these risks and make a plan. That's what my eight Tax-Zero strategies are all about. That's why I want to share them with as many people as possible.

CHAPTER 3

Strategy #1:
Shift Your Tax Allocation

One year in my childhood, I got a new bicycle for Christmas. I was so excited to have my own ride. Freedom! Then, one day, I left my bike out in the rain. I kind of forgot about it after the initial thrill had worn off. When I went to ride it the next time, it was so rusty. A hard lesson: where you place your assets matters.

The saying is, "The easiest way to guarantee a higher rate of return on investments is not what you own but where you own it." The easiest way to make more money is to pay less in taxes.

So, the secret is out: I'm not a big fan of relying on retirement accounts to build wealth. Conventional wisdom has taught us that we should stick our aggressive money or our growth money in our retirement accounts. Retirement accounts are for the long term. Our after-tax or savings accounts should be used for emergencies.

Simply put, that rule of thumb can be expensive and downright wrong for many people, especially once you get into retirement. The problem with that philosophy is you're utilizing retirement accounts improperly. Inside a retirement account, everything that you pull out will get taxed at your current income. So, if you have stocks and growth in there, everything is taxable. In the after-tax account, if you have CDs or money market savings, that interest is taxed on your current income as well. By relying so heavily on retirement accounts, all of your assets are being taxed at your current income.

You've been stashing money away like this for years. What can you do? By switching where you own the assets as you get close to retirement and into retirement, you can significantly save and utilize the free-tax benefits the IRS provides.

Making The Shift

Here's how it works. Let's say there are two couples, Jim and Joan Smith and Bob and Barbara Jones, who live on the same street and are the same age. They are all sixty-five. Both couples have $100,000 invested. The Smiths have it in their IRA, and the Joneses have some in their IRA and some in their non-qualified after-tax account.

The year is 2022, and the market takes a tumble and is down 20 percent. They both have to take $10,000 out of their investments. The Smith's nest egg, in an IRA, is down to $80,000, and they take $10,000 out. The Joneses, with their after-tax account, were able to harvest the loss from the stock going down. The Joneses came out ahead. Both couples had the same investment, the same dollar amount. One in an IRA, and one in an after-tax account. Both got the same $10,000 out, but one pays more taxes, and the other got a tax rebate of sorts with a tax deduction.

Wait, what? How does that math add up?

The Joneses made smart moves to save on taxes in this situation. You can do something similar without much hassle. The idea is to adjust where you keep your investments to pay fewer taxes.

Here's a basic plan: Take the investments that are likely to grow and generate fewer taxes and move them from your retirement account (IRA) to your regular investment account or Roth. Then, put the investments that could lead to higher taxes—like interest-paying investments, CDs, bonds, or frequently traded assets—into your retirement account.

Now, imagine you have a professional manager handling your investments. Sometimes, they might make decisions that result in capital gains (profits) or short-term gains in your retirement account. Here's how to save money and not change what you're investing in, just where you're investing it. Move your safer investments—retirement savings and growth-focused investments—to your regular after-tax account. This shift allows you to take advantage of tax benefits provided by the IRS.

There are three significant tax benefits:

1. **Capital Gains:** When you own stocks in an IRA, any profit you make from selling them is subject to a lower tax rate than your regular income. So, it's better to keep these stocks outside your IRA to enjoy this tax advantage.

2. **Claiming Losses:** Stocks don't always increase in value; they can also go down. You can save money in taxes by keeping these kinds of investments outside your retirement account and claiming any losses.

3. **Step Up:** The last benefit is known as "step up in basis." What does that mean? According to the Tax Foundation,[4] "The step-up in basis provision adjusts the value, or 'cost basis,' of an inherited asset (stocks, bonds, real estate, etc.) when it is passed on, after death.

"This often reduces the capital gains tax owed by the recipient. The cost basis receives a 'step-up' to its fair market value, or the price at which the good would be sold or purchased in a fair market. This eliminates the capital gain that occurred between the original purchase of the asset and the heir's acquisition, reducing the heir's tax liability."

Let's say you own a stock, you buy it at one dollar, and it grows to $100,000 in your IRA. When you pass away, your heirs are paying taxes on at least $100,000. If you owned that same investment in your regular account, that gain would be stepped up when you pass away, meaning your heirs could use that money tax-free. So, in essence, having your growth investments inside your IRA account causes you to pay current income taxes on everything. Stepped up in basis allows you to move those into your after-tax account.

	Tax treatment of expected returns	Taxable	Tax-deferred	Tax-exempt
Municipal securities and municipal mutual funds	Generally exempt	✔ More appropriate	✔ Less appropriate	✔ Less appropriate
Equity securities held long-term for growth	Taxed at long-term capital gain rates	✔ More appropriate	✔ Appropriate	✔ Appropriate
Equity index funds/ETFs (other than REITs)		✔ More appropriate	✔ Appropriate	✔ Appropriate
Tax-managed mutual funds		✔ More appropriate	✔ Less appropriate	✔ Less appropriate
Real estate investment trusts (REITs)	Generally, 80% of income taxed at ordinary rates; 20% tax-exempt	✔ Appropriate	✔ More appropriate	✔ More appropriate
High-turnover stock mutual funds that deliver effectively all returns as short-term capital gains	Taxed at ordinary income rates	✔ Less appropriate	✔ More appropriate	✔ More appropriate
Fully taxable bonds and bond funds (i.e., corporates)		✔ Less appropriate	✔ More appropriate	✔ More appropriate

✔ More appropriate ✔ Appropriate ✔ Less appropriate

https://www.fidelity.com/viewpoints/investing-ideas/asset-location-lower-taxes

CHAPTER 4

Strategy #2: Harvest Your Tax Losses

This next strategy is something like cutting down a rosebush to encourage new growth. You are losing growth to gain more in the future. If you own stocks or appreciable assets in a regular account—not your 401(k), IRA, or Roth—you'll realize capital gains when you sell them.

Or, as we've described in the previous chapter, to avoid the capital gains hit, you can realize a tax loss. For example, if you sell an investment that you bought for $10,000 and you sold for $7,000, that's a $3,000 loss. The IRS allows you to claim up to $3,000 a year of capital losses against your income. Furthermore, you can claim as many losses as you have capital gains. If you have another position that you made a $20,000 capital gain on, you can sell another position at a $20,000 loss and wipe out that gain altogether.

Here's how this works: Imagine two neighbors who make the same income. They both have $100,000 in their after-tax or non-qualified account and are invested in the same S&P 500 Index. The market went down 3 percent that year, and so both of their investments are now worth $97,000. One neighbor does nothing and stays with their $97,000 investment with no tax implications. The other client sells the position at $97,000 and buys it back. This can't be done willy-nilly. There are certain rules about how to buy back investments, so you must stay within those rules. The result is that this neighbor realized a $3,000 loss on their taxes. When it was all said and done, both still owned $97,000 of the same investment. However, one person was able to claim the $3,000 loss on their tax return, which reduced their taxable income by $3,000.*

**Disclaimer: This is for illustration educational purposes only. Please see a qualified financial advisor to handle a transaction like this properly.*

**Further disclaimer: This could incur what's called a wash-sale rule. It's an IRS rule. There are ways to implement the strategy effectively or properly. Consult a qualified financial advisor and explicitly acknowledge the wash-sale rule.*

So, tax-loss harvesting is simply selling investments that have lost money and claiming that on your tax return.

Let's dig into this a little further. If you have losses and you can claim them, you can and should be looking to claim up to $3,000 against your current income. This is a good strategy because current income taxes are higher than capital gains taxes. So, if I claim a $3,000 loss today on a stock, I have a $3,000 loss on my income at a tax bracket of, let's say, 24 percent. If I didn't buy the stock back, and it grows $3,000 down the road, and I sell it, I'd have to pay back that $3,000 in taxes even though I still have the same investment. It went from ten to seven and back to ten.

The difference is that $3,000 gain is paid in the future, when taxes may be higher, but that $3,000 gain is taxed at capital gains rates, which is lower than current income. So, you just had kind of an arbitrage (the simultaneous buying and selling of securities, currency, or commodities) in taxes. You got a claim against income, which is higher, and you had to pay it back at capital gains, which is at a lower rate.

What about when you have gains in your positions? The second strategy is for a situation in which you have massive capital gains. Maybe you sold a position and had gains. Now, you want to look inside your portfolio to see if you can eat into as much of those gains as possible. With this strategy, you are counterbalancing the big stock sale that was a winner with losers.

The third strategy is to utilize tax-loss harvesting to get your income lower, so that we can do more of some of the other strategies. So, if you can claim $3,000 in losses this year, we can contribute or convert $3,000 from an IRA to a Roth for free. That's not really a big number, but it is something.

Using any of these strategies for tax harvesting helps get you toward Tax Zero by simply claiming against income and/or claiming against gains.

Tax Loss Harvesting Details

	Capital Gain With No Tax Loss Harvest	Capital Gain With Tax Loss Harvest
Zoom Cost Basis 4/1/2020	200,000.00	200,000.00
Zoom Sales Price 12/31/2022	400,000.00	400,000.00
Capital Gain Realized	**$200,000.00**	**$200,000.00**
ABC Mobile Cost Basis 1/1/2007		1,200,000.00
ABC Mobile Sales Price 12/31/2022		600,000.00
Loss Harvested	**$ -**	**$(600,000.00)**
Net Capital Gain(Loss)	200,000.00	(400,000.00)
Capital Gain Tax Rate	20%	0%
Current Tax Liability	40,000.00	-
Tax Savings via Tax Loss Harvest		**40,000.00**
Net Capital Loss Carryforward for Future Use		**(400,000.00)**
Cash Proceeds from Sale of ABC Mobile		**600,000.00***

*Use the cash proceeds from the sale to repurchase the same stock and reestablish a lower cost basis for future gains

CHAPTER 5

Strategy #3: Take Advantage Of Permanent Life Insurance

Your whole life (pun intended), you have been warned against buying into the myths of permanent life insurance. Or maybe you have heard something about how permanent life insurance can be useful in some instances. But the details are murky. When it comes to the subject of permanent life insurance, most people have one or both of those experiences. I want to dispel the myths and provide you with some clarity.

While this isn't a strategy for everyone, it is something that the likes of Walt Disney and JCPenney did. They leveraged the power of permanent life insurance. When he couldn't secure financing, Disney used the cash value of his policy to make his Disneyland theme park dreams a reality. During the Great Depression, JCPenney used it to meet payroll and other expenses until the stores regained their footing.[5] The lesson here is not to take risks with your cash value but to leverage it wisely as money that you are borrowing from yourself.

Conventional financial planning wisdom would have you buy affordable term insurance and invest the difference. By taking that path, you might miss out on the tax advantages of permanent life insurance.

Most people buy life insurance to provide a death benefit for the protection of their spouse, partner, children, and other heirs. The death benefit is tax-free. On that basis alone, life insurance, in general, is a part of the tax-free discussion.

I am more concerned about when the clients are living versus when they pass away. How does this fit into the tax-free discussion? Because there are certain strategies around permanent life insurance that allow you to accumulate and use a portion of your funds tax-free.

You'll want to weigh the pros and cons of this strategy carefully. Leveraging permanent life insurance is an amazing strategy, but it comes with extra costs. First and foremost, the death benefit costs money. If you don't need a death benefit to keep your family whole after you pass away, that cost may outweigh the benefit. You may be able to accomplish the same strategy without having to pay for life insurance.

Here is the part you may have heard about before. Permanent life insurance can be helpful because it allows you to tap into the cash value of your life insurance. Again, there are caveats to this. First, are you maxing out your Roth IRA? Are you maxing out your HSA? Have you used some of these other strategies first? We typically recommend prioritizing the other options before looking at life insurance.

Think of this as more of a secondary strategy. We view life insurance, a lot of times, as a one-trick pony. These restrictions, complexities, and handcuffs are why we view this as a secondary strategy.

The power of this strategy is in the cash value, the money you have available to you right now. That's why you want to overpay—not just put in the monthly minimum set up under the policy but a larger chunk—to build up a cash value in the policy. That cash value grows tax-deferred, and if used properly and distributed properly, you can tap back into that cash value tax-free.

I call the cash value inside of a life insurance policy "half money." Yes, that cash value is in the policy, and yes, you can go in there and get it. If you pull all the cash value out, you lose the death benefit. The death benefit is there, but if you die, a lot of the cash value is wasted. That's why I say it's half money. You typically want to use life insurance for either cash value or life insurance. If you're counting on both, then you're usually overpaying for that benefit. This is not a strategy unique to me. Other advisors talk about the power of permanent life insurance. The process and the value proposition are pretty clear-cut but understand the restrictions and be careful.

You can access the cash value in your policy tax-free in two ways. The first option is that you are allowed to remove all premiums paid into the policy. For example, if you paid $100,000 of premiums into a policy and the cash value had grown to $150,000. You would be able to pull the first $100,000 out tax-free. Any additional withdrawals would result in taxable income. The second option is by taking a loan against the cash value. This allows you access to the cash while also maintaining the death benefit for your heirs. It also may be accessed in a way that you would never have to repay the loan. This can be a great option for large, one-time expenses. The key is that you will want to monitor this loan each year to ensure the policy stays in force.

There are pros and cons to each strategy. The power of Tax Zero is to understand the tools you have available and use them properly. A hammer is good for nailing nails. A saw is good for cutting a board in half, but don't use the saw to hammer nails, and don't use a hammer to break a board apart. Find the right use and the right combination of the tool of permanent life insurance and the other Tax-Zero strategies, and you will be prepared for retirement and enjoy that time of life with less stress.

Life Insurance Details

- Permanent life insurance builds cash value, a reserve of money you can access while alive.
- Cash value grows tax deferred, only taxable when you take out the monies.
- You can withdraw up to your premium payments tax-free and pay tax on any gains above and beyond the premiums.
- Can access your cash value through a loan and borrow against it without having to pay tax on the gains. If you pass with a remaining loan balance, the death benefit pays it off and the heirs receive the remainder income tax-free.
- Life insurance death benefit is always tax free to its beneficiaries.
- No income limits or limits on how much you put into it.

	Whole Life Insurance
Average Annual Premiums Paid	$13,200.00
Years Paid	30
Total Investment In Life Insurance	**$396,000.00**
Average Annual Rate Of Return	2.50%
Total Value After Thirty Years	**$581,613.00**
Total Tax-Deferred Growth Over Thirty Years	$185,613.00
Capital Gain Tax Rate	15%
Total Capital Gain Tax Deferred	**$27,841.95**
Death Benefit Paid	500,000.00
Tax Rate	22%
Total Tax Savings On Death Benefit	**$110,000.00**

CHAPTER 6

Strategy #4: Control Taxes With Annuities

Here's my hot take on annuities: 80 percent of annuities are wrong for 80 percent of the people. Most are bad for all the people. Typically, they have high fees, which could be 3 to 4 percent a year. They lock you up. They lure you in with the siren song of tax deferral. But if you need access, you can't get it. They offer benefits, but do you need all of them? For instance, you will be paying for a death benefit that you might not need.

With all this downside and the fact that fewer than one-fifth of households between ages forty and eighty-five even own annuities,[6] why talk about them? But all that doesn't mean there is no place for annuities. Annuities can fill a void. There are a lot of competitive annuities benefits that could be attractive. The two most common areas are fixed interest and lifetime income annuities. If you can get a fixed-rate annuity paying higher interest than current bonds, it is worth considering.

The biggest benefit of an annuity is tax control, not tax deferral. Note that we're talking here about controlling taxes, not necessarily avoiding them. Let's look at how it plays out to control taxes rather than defer them, using annuities as that instrument.

Here's how deferral works. So, I've got $200,000 in my checking/savings account for short-term spending and larger emergencies. I've invested in CDs, bonds, and things like that which pay interest and are then taxed at my current income. By utilizing an annuity, I can make it a fixed interest, just like I do with a CD for a term that's similar—two years or so. The difference is that the interest that a fixed annuity pays is built up in the policy, and you won't pay taxes on it until you pull the money out.

Once you pull it out, you will pay taxes just like you would with a normal CD. We see a lot of people buy annuities, and then they defer it for a lifetime just because they're trying to avoid taxes. That strategy might be right for you. But what I like about annuities is being able to control my taxes. If I can take money out of a bond or bond fund that's being taxed at current income and stick it into a fixed-rate annuity that is paying similar interest or even higher, I can then avoid paying unnecessary taxes each year when I do not need the money. The annuity would allow me to pull out the interest only when I choose, which means I will only pay taxes when I use those funds.

Switching from traditional bonds to annuities usually immediately reduces your current tax liability, getting closer to Tax Zero. The goal is not to defer this interest indefinitely because you or your beneficiaries will eventually have to pay it. The goal with deferral is to allow you to do more of our other strategies. Reducing your taxable interest income could allow you to convert more funds to a Roth while not paying more taxes. Remember, annuities can be useful, but they have their drawbacks. You will have to pull money out of it eventually, or you should, and it will likely be taxed at a higher rate. The good news is that you control that date. For IRAs, the government controls the date. So, we like to use annuities to buy ourselves some time to strategically use the accounts that have mandates while we can.

Annuity Example Details

	Investment Vehicle	
	Annuity	Bond
Rate Of Return/Interest Rate	3%	3%
Amount Invested	100,000.00	100,000.00
Annual Growth At 3%	3,000.00	3,000.00
Annual Taxable Growth Required To Be Reported	$-	$3,000.00
Tax Bracket	22%	22%
Current Tax Liability	$-	$660.00
Tax Deferred Via Annuity	**$660.00**	

Annuity allows you to control when and how you pay tax

The Problem With Parking Your Money In CDs And Bonds

This is what you've been taught to do: put your after-tax money into savings. So, you may have them in bonds or bond funds. Say you have $500,000 in bonds. The bond funds make 4 percent interest. That 4 percent interest on $500,000 adds up to $20,000 a year in interest. Awesome! Except, because it's in a non-qualified account, whether you spend it or not, whether you reinvest it or not, you're going to get a 1099 from your account that says you earned $20,000 in taxable interest.

By transitioning that $500,000 to a fixed-rate annuity—let's say the fixed-rate annuity is also paying 4 percent—you're still making $20,000 a year in interest. But your taxable interest went down by $20,000 because that annuity is tax deferred.

And here is a sneak peek at Tax-Zero Strategy Number Seven: By going $20,000 lower (by not having that $20,000 in taxable interest), you can convert $20,000 of your IRA to a Roth. So now you've got $20,000 more than you did in an account that will forever grow tax-free, and you technically didn't pay any extra taxes this year to do it. You still made the same interest on that money, but because you deferred it, you added $20,000 more into your Roth account.

CHAPTER 7

Strategy #5:
Give Wisely To Charity

As kids, we would receive a weekly allowance for completing our chores. Five dollars a week was the pay, which at that time could buy a kid some primo candy and comic books. This came to about one dollar and fifty cents an hour, but we will not get into child labor laws at this time. The problem was after I received the five dollars, my parents would make me allocate 10 percent of that money to savings and 10 percent to giving/tithing. This only left me with three dollars to spend for all my efforts, barely enough to buy a pack of baseball cards. That 20 percent withheld from the top hurt at first, but as I grew older, the value became clear.

Giving is not about receiving some kind of reward. We don't give to get. Charitable contributions are a personal choice based on your interests and personal connection to a cause you find worthwhile.

That being said, if you are actively giving, ensure you do it wisely. The Tax Act of 2018 really hurt those who give charitably. According to the Tax Policy Center,[7] "Overall, the Tax Cut and Jobs Act (TCJA) reduced the marginal tax benefit of giving to charity by more than 30 percent in 2018, raising the after-tax cost of donating by about 7 percent."

So, in this environment, what does it mean to give wisely to charity? In this chapter, I'll cover three strategies: first, give to donor-advised funds. You can also lump your charitable contributions and qualified charitable distributions (donate your RMDs).

While the TCJA reduces people's taxes by and large, the mechanism to accomplish this was by increasing the standard deduction. The standard deduction is the amount of money you can make that the government allows to be tax-free, and the tax cut doubled that number. So far, so good; that's now twice as much money that you get tax-free. Sounds very Tax-Zero–friendly, right? But that's not the end of the story.

The problem is that your ability to itemize has decreased dramatically. Why is that? Because your itemizations must exceed the standard deduction to qualify as a further deduction. Typical retirees and people looking to retire in the not-so-distant future are losing many of the typical itemized deductions. Your children are no longer dependent, and your mortgage interest is probably low because you don't have much left to pay off. Your ability to deduct decreases as you get older. So, this standard deduction increase had a double-whammy effect on charitable donations for those nearing retirement.

The good news is, according to a 2023 Giving USA annual report, the TCJA does not seem to have significantly dampened people's enthusiasm for charitable giving.[8] However, for the goal of Tax Zero, it's important to know how to maximize your giving while maximizing your tax benefits. With that in mind, here are three primary strategies.

Giving Strategy #1: Lump Sum Giving

The first strategy is lumping your giving into one major contribution instead of a little bit here and there. Let's say throughout a given year, you give $5,000 to your church or charity. If you give $5,000 a year, you're still nowhere near your standard deduction. You'll get the standard deduction but won't be able to deduct this $5,000 contribution. What if, instead, you took five years' worth of that contribution—so $25,000—and you gave it all in one year to that church or charity? You'd be able to claim $25,000, which would allow you to itemize your taxes this year. Then for the next four years, you would take a standard deduction, but at least you got something in return for that $25,000.

The problem with this strategy is you need to give all the money all at once. For such a generous gift, you want to choose a cause for whom you will continue to have a strong affinity. Also, you've given this large amount, so you might feel the need to steel yourself against requests from organizations and causes you care about. You gave a substantial contribution to one place, but friends will have birthday fundraisers for causes, and you'll have new causes you care about. Nothing stops you from making these smaller donations, but understand you'll have to manage that along with that larger lump sum gift.

Giving Strategy #2: Donor-Advised Funds

The better way of lumping those contributions together is to use what we call a "donor-advised fund." This is an account where you can lump multiple years' worth of contributions into one year. Using that same $25,000 from the previous example allows you to itemize $25,000 on your taxes, which will get you an itemized deduction.

The great thing about a donor-advised fund is you don't have to disperse the money all at once. You can dole those funds out for as long as they last. You do eventually have to give all the funds away, but you can use it essentially like a personal checkbook to give to your faith community or charities. This strategy allows you to get that deduction without having to give it all away in one year. The one catch is that the organizations you give to need to be registered 501(c) charities recognized by the IRS.

Another way you can use donor-advised funds is an option when you have highly appreciated assets. This might be a stock you purchased long ago that has appreciated dramatically. Let's say you bought $1,000 worth of stock and now it's now worth $25,000. If you were to sell that stock today, you would realize a $24,000 capital gain. Many choose to do this. They may sell a position or get taxable income to then give to their faith community or charities. A donor-advised fund allows you to donate a highly appreciated investment. So that same stock, if you sold it, you'd have a $24,000 capital gain, but you can donate that $25,000 stock directly to your donor-advised fund.

This has twice the impact: First, you get a $25,000 itemized deduction this year. Second, you avoid the $24,000 capital gain. So, you saved twice by making that contribution. Donor-advised funds are ideal or even better if you have highly appreciated stocks to donate.

Giving Strategy #3: Qualified Charitable Distributions

The third strategy is what's called a qualified charitable distribution or QCD. The nice thing about a QCD is it's essentially free and uncomplicated. You don't have to create some entity like a charitable remainder trust. A QCD can be set up at a low cost or no cost. Rather than setting up a trust and paying attorneys' fees, you are simply setting up an account, just like you would an IRA.

If you're over seventy and a half years old, the government allows you to make a direct contribution or contribution to a religious institution or charity from your qualified accounts, like your IRA or 401(k). So, you can take money from a qualified account and contribute to your favorite charity while avoiding the taxation of the distribution, which is, in effect, a tax break.

We have a long-time client, a woman now in her seventies. She gives roughly $1,000 to a favorite charity every year. Being in her seventies, her IRA has a required minimum distribution (RMD), which in her situation is $8,000 a year. In past years, before working with us, she would take $8,000 out and pay tax on it as income. From what remained after taxes, she gave the $1,000, which is nowhere near the standard deduction, so she was getting no benefit for that.

The simple strategy we recommended was, "Hey, you're required to take $8,000 out. You want to give $1,000 to your church or charity. Let's just have that money go directly from your qualified account to the charity." Just remember to get written acknowledgment of the gift from the charity.

The difference in giving it directly was that it reduced her taxable income by $1,000 in her tax bracket. That was $230 in savings for effectively doing nothing different than what she was doing before, just modifying how she did it. So QCDs are especially good for those who are seventy-and-a-half years old or above and/or give amounts that are less than $4,000 or $5,000 a year. Because if you were only given, let's say, a thousand dollars a year and you wanted to do a donor-advised fund, you'd have to effectively put twenty years' worth in there, and people may not have that kind of money. So, a QCD is the easiest and simplest strategy out there.

QCD Example Details

	Single RMD Without QCD	Single RMD With QCD
Annual RMD Amount	$8,000.00	$8,000.00
RMD Breakdown		
Distribution	8,000.00	6,000.00
Charitable Contribution	-	2,000.00
RMD Satisfied	**$8,000.00**	**$8,000.00**
Taxable RMD	8,000.00	6,000.00
Tax Bracket	22%	22%
Tax Liability	**$1,760.00**	**$1,320.00**
Tax Savings Via QCD		**440.00***

* Tax Savings resulted not in how much they donated to charity, but the vehicle by which they donated.

Giving to your faith community or an organization you volunteer with or have some other close connection—we do those things because we want to. But having these strategies in place can make giving that much easier, with less—or even zero—tax burden.

CHAPTER 8

Strategy #6:
Save With A Healthcare Spending Account

As a kid, I used to love a good buffet, especially one with an ice cream bar—all the toppings I could imagine were there! Now, when I go to an ice cream shop, I add up in my head what I would be paying for that ice cream sundae I created as a kid. You've got to pay extra for all the toppings. That sundae would cost a fortune.

In healthcare, extras—and even the basics—can also cost a fortune. Unlike ice cream toppings, many of these expenses are not just nice to have but critical to health and recovery when we are sick or injured. Yet healthcare expenses can be financially devastating when a medical emergency happens. That's why it's so important to be prepared for the unexpected with good health insurance. Putting money aside to pay for any medical expenses not covered by insurance is important, too. That's where a Healthcare Spending Account (HSA) comes in. An HSA is like a sundae with all the toppings—at no extra cost.

Most advisors encourage people to contribute to an HSA to pay for health expenses each year tax-free. You contribute to the account and use the balance each year, and there is no tax penalty on that money. It's like the benefit of an IRA plus a Roth, meaning you get a deduction, and you pull it out tax-free, but it's limited to just health expenses.

That's basically all an HSA can be used for, right? *Wrong.* Here is where the potential of an HSA gets interesting.

I just learned about this strategy recently, and I call it the holy grail of zero tax. Writing in *Forbes*,[9] David Rodeck calls it a "hat trick," meaning there are three distinct tax benefits. He writes, "Contributions to your account are made pre-tax, lowering your taxable income today; investments grow tax-free while they're kept in the account; and withdrawals are free of income tax, as long as you use the money for qualified medical expenses."

It's a deduction *and* can be tax-free. The challenge is not everyone qualifies or has access to a large enough HSA. According to the IRS, you can qualify for an HSA under the following conditions:

1. You are covered under a high deductible health plan (what qualifies as "high deductible" is described in current IRS guidelines)
2. You have only health coverage permitted under current guidelines
3. You aren't enrolled in Medicare
4. You can't be claimed as a dependent on someone else's tax return

Healthcare spending doesn't have to be used up ("use it or lose it") like the Personal Spending Account (PSA) or Flexible Spending Account (FSA). The benefit of an HSA, if you're eligible and have a high-deductible plan, is that you can make contributions to this HSA account just like you do an IRA or other spending accounts.

Now, can you use HSA money for any healthcare expense? Should you keep the receipts for all your Band-Aids and cough medicine? Will Botox injections count? Not everything is eligible to be expensed through your HSA. An HSA will only cover expenses that your health insurance would typically cover. If your health insurance paid for a portion of it, then traditionally, you could claim your portion as an HSA expense. If it's an elective procedure, like "I'm getting a face lift," no, your health insurance doesn't cover that, so you're not going to get reimbursed for that.

So, the good news is that you can use an HSA for qualified health-related expenses tax-free.

However, there is more you need to understand about how HSAs work.

HSA Does Not Spell "IRA"

While most people use the HSA to pay for health-related expenses as they occur, what happens if money accumulates over time in an HSA? Nothing requires that you empty an HSA each year. You can invest in your HSA account just as you would in your 401(k) or IRA. That money has the potential to grow as you contribute year after year.

The problem is a lot of people grow their HSAs, and then at retirement, they treat it a lot like an IRA. Once you are fifty-nine-and-a-half years old, you can cash out your HSA balance, but it's going to be taxed because it wasn't used for healthcare.

A better strategy is to contribute to your HSA, use it as little as possible if you can avoid it, and treat it as a retirement account. However, if you save up your expenses and keep good documentation, the IRS allows you to use medical expenses from previous years as justification to pull this money out in retirement. So, you could save all your expenses over the next twenty years, and then when you retire, completely cash out this HSA 100 percent tax-free, which effectively gives you IRA account benefits plus a Roth account.

Here's the power of this strategy: Say you have contributed $6,000 a year to an HSA and never touched it. You put the money in the account, and the investment grows. When you retire, you have $300,000 in your HSA account. The crucial step here is that you have saved up all your eligible expenses over the years. For the first three years of retirement, you pull out $100,000 a year, 100 percent tax-free, because you can document the expenses this covers. That is an extreme example, but if you have a paper trail, this is money you can claim tax-free.

This is an approach that takes discipline. The standard approach to an HSA is to use it exclusively for medical expenses, paying out and replenishing the funds each year. But "stockpiling" your expenses and paying them out after retirement is the truly Tax-Zero option. The challenge is, can you pay for medical expenses out of pocket and contribute to, but not touch, your HSA? By paying out of pocket, you can itemize a massive health bill in retirement. We'll dig further into the power of a Roth in the next chapter, but with this strategy, you can convert hundreds of thousands of dollars from your 401(k) to a Roth by using up that tax-free HSA money in the first few years of retirement.

All of the above reasons are why I call this the holy grail of Tax Zero in retirement. It saved you on taxes. It's the best account, period.

Below is a chart that compares HSA with Roth contributions. In the scenario below, the tax savings with the HSA are nearly triple that of the Roth, so you can see why others and I use superlatives like "holy grail" and "hat trick."

Roth vs. HSA Example Details

- Facts: Client has $90,000 of annual income
- Scenario 1: Maxing out Roth Contribution each year
- Scenario 2: Maxing out HSA contribution & investing the funds

	Scenario 1	Scenario 2
	Roth Contribution	**HSA Contribution**
Annual Contribution:	$4,150	$4,150
Years	10	10
Total Contributed Over Ten Years:	**$41,500**	**$41,500**
Annual Growth Assumed:	8.00%	8.00%
Total Value After Ten years:	64,928.77	64,928.77
Non-Taxable Growth:	**23,428.77**	**23,428.77**
Tax Rate:	22%	22%
Tax Savings From Growth:	**5,154.33**	**5,154.33**
Tax Deduction Allowed Over Ten years:		41,500.00
Federal Tax Rate:		22
Tax Savings From HSA Contribution:		**$9,130.00**
Total Tax Savings Over 10 years:	**$5,154.33**	**$14,284.33**

In this example, we show the additional benefits of an HSA account versus what most people believe is the best tax-planning account, the Roth IRA. In this scenario, the client has the option to contribute to an HSA or a Roth account, contributing $4,150 per year. The contributions would be the same over a ten-year period, and at the same asset growth rate, they would end up being the same value over that time. The tax savings on any distributions would be equal to a Roth as well as an HSA.

The biggest differentiating factor is the ability to take deductions when putting money into the account. For the Roth IRA, you get no tax deduction for putting that money in. However, with an HSA you do and can qualify for tax deduction.

In this example, with the same person at a 22 percent tax rate, the savings from the HSA contribution would equal over $9,000. The Roth IRA can't compete with that. So, the impact over a ten-year period for the same person with the same tax bracket, the tax benefit of an HSA could almost be triple that of a Roth IRA.

Does that make an IRA a terrible way to save for retirement? No. IRAs are excellent for tax-deferred retirement savings. But if you are eligible for an HSA and can follow this strategy, as you can see by these calculations, it could be a much bigger benefit, which is why we usually say start with an HSA.

CHAPTER 9

Strategy #7:
Convert To A Roth IRA

When *Terminator 2* came out, my mom went to a conference. She rarely went out of town, but she went to a conference for teachers. The last thing she told my dad as she headed out the door was, "Henry, do not take the kids to see *Terminator 2*."

The first thing my dad did on Friday night was announce, "All right, kids, let's go see *Terminator 2*!"

If you are unfamiliar, the Terminator movies are all about how the robots are out to get us. You know, terminate. That movie sticks in my head, mainly because we were doing something "illegal," at least against my mom's laws. It was a cool movie. I hope one day the robots come down and blow away our debt instead of us. What I definitely don't want is for the government to terminate the ability to convert a regular IRA into a Roth IRA.

Don't Terminate My Conversion!

Creating an in-depth tax plan requires real talk. To balance the ledger, whether we are talking about a family budget, a business, or local, state, and federal government, there are two options: raise revenue or cut spending.

Here is one place where your personal budget and the US federal budget intersect. Money coming in from matured IRAs with minimum required distributions represents one of the biggest sources of additional tax revenue for the federal government. Taxes are your biggest expense in retirement.

Recently, we came close to losing the ability to convert a standard IRA to a Roth. How was that? Build Back Better was a bill passed by the House of Representatives, but it did not make it through the Senate. The White House wanted to pass an infrastructure bill. However, one of the biggest ways they found to pay for Build Back Better and all these trillions of dollars was to eliminate the ability of Americans to convert to a Roth. It would save them trillions.

They were going to, ahem, terminate our ability to convert to a Roth. Thank goodness, another version of the bill eventually passed, and that didn't happen because here's what happens when you convert to a Roth.

As of this writing, converting to a Roth is still possible, so it makes great sense to consider doing this.

Because we see such compelling evidence that many retirees will be taxed at a higher rate (because taxes trend upward, not downward), it makes great sense to convert to a Roth IRA. When we do tax planning, we find most would benefit from converting to a Roth, but most should not convert everything. For many, converting even small portions can have a big impact. To be clear, you will owe taxes on the money you convert, but you can take tax-free withdrawals from the Roth IRA in the future.

In a 2024 article in the *New York Times*[10] that echoes several Tax-Zero strategies, Brian J. O'Connor writes:

> *Some retirees might benefit from taking the tax hit that comes from transferring tax-deferred money in a traditional I.R.A. or 401(k) to a Roth I.R.A., which makes all future withdrawals tax-free. Retirees younger than 73 might want to delay Social Security and pension payments early in retirement in order to deplete I.R.A.s and other accounts before R.M.D.s kick in. Still, another strategy is to send R.M.D. payments directly to charity if you don't need the income, which can cut your tax bill. In all cases, you'll need to decide whether to have income tax withheld from Social Security, pension payments, and account withdrawals or to make quarterly estimated tax payments.*

It is important to understand the five-year rule around Roth conversions. Money going into the Roth is usually the last fund you want to use to maximize tax-free growth. Make sure you still have funds in an emergency fund to cover expenses for the next few years so you do not lose a portion of that benefit.

Imagine your dear grandmother passed away. She planned well and lived a good, long life to over one hundred years old. She got to travel and spend on herself and her family exactly as she wanted. She then passed away peacefully in her sleep.

As part of your inheritance, Grandma bequeathed you an amazing property right on the beach. However, she played a little trick. She made you 80 percent owner and your cousin 20 percent owner. And I'm not talking about just any cousin. This is the cousin who hadn't been invited to Christmas in thirty years. This is not the stuff of which an amicable partnership is built. The good news is you can buy your cousin out for 20 percent. The bad news: If you put this off, after three years, your cousin's cut goes to 25 percent. You can still buy him out, and he has no say whatsoever, but it's going to cost 25 percent.

When do you buy your cousin out? As soon as possible. Why do you do it? It's common sense, an easy decision. Number one: because 20 percent is less than 25 percent. Secondly, that beach lot, on average, will increase in value yearly. So, not only are you paying a higher percentage, but you're paying a higher percentage on a bigger dollar amount. The last thing is—forget about the money—this is the cousin you don't invite to Christmas anymore. You don't want anything to do with them. If you own the beach lot with them, they have some say in how to manage it. You want them out of your life. So, you buy 'em out today.

That is similar to what the government is doing with your retirement account. Let's pretend that tomorrow, you go out to your mailbox and get your 401k statement. You open it, and it says you now have one million dollars in it. Great!

That statement is lying to you. You do not own one hundred percent of the account; you "co-own" it with the government if you are in the 24 percent tax bracket. That statement should say yes, there is a million dollars in there, but at least $240,000 of it belongs to the government. If you try to cash it all out today, close to half of it goes to the government.

Like your cousin and the beach lot, you co-own the retirement account with the government. So, if you believe taxes will go up and their cut will be higher in the future, when is the best time to buy your cousin out of your beach property or buy out the government of your retirement? Today.

One caveat to this story. Unlike the beach lot, most people should not buy out the entire account from the government, but if you think their cut is going up, then you should consider buying the government out for a portion of your standard Roth or 401(k).

CHAPTER 10

Strategy #8: Utilize Tax-Free (Sort Of) Bonds

Early in my career, when I focused on selling CDs, I would occasionally run into a few peculiar people. They would have all of their money in CDs at the bank, earning around 3 to 4 percent. I would show them how they could buy CDs and earn over 6 percent. I would be ecstatic because, for many, this would mean they would earn thousands of dollars each year while staying completely FDIC-insured.

Yet, some with whom I shared this news came back and said, "Josh, that seems great, but I am going to pass." Dumbfounded, I would follow up, wondering why anyone would skip this amazing opportunity. The response was, "If I make more interest, I am going to have to pay more taxes." This was in the South, so maybe they were basically saying,

"Bless your heart," as a way to politely end the conversation. I wondered what the problem was in paying extra taxes if I had an extra $10,000 in earned interest.

This polite but firm resistance made me dig deeper beyond CDs. The next investment I added to my arsenal was municipal bonds. Municipal bonds are debt securities issued by local governments to raise money for projects and to fund day-to-day operations,[11] which can be federally tax-free or taxable depending on the type.

The biggest benefit of these bonds is that they can be federal- and sometimes even state-tax-free. I came to realize that this is a great way to earn good interest and save some on taxes. It is a win-win.

So, let's say you have $200,000 in your checking and savings accounts. A CD is earning 3 percent interest. CD interest is taxed each year as you earn it. Instead of buying another CD, you could buy a municipal bond, and let's say it's making 3 percent, but it's federally tax-free. Both vehicles are earning the interest, but with the bond, you are not paying federal taxes. That's a Tax-Zero strategy with no penalty and no taxes to pay.

The problem with municipal bonds is that while municipal bonds can be federal- and state-tax-free, they can still lead you to pay Social Security taxes. The government includes "tax-free" municipal interest as a factor on whether your Social Security is tax-free.

Municipal Bonds And Social Security Taxes

Let's say you have $100,000,000 in South Carolina bonds. If you live in this state, that money would be tax-free for federal and state income. However, you are earning a lot of interest on that money. It could be $400,000 a year of interest that needs to be put into the calculation of whether your Social Security is taxable or not.

And so, you could literally have a $0 income with Social Security, and 85 percent of your Social Security is going to be taxable because of that bond interest. It's not taxable, but it counts in taxation. In an article on Investopedia,[12] Thom Tracy warns, "If you receive Social Security, your bond interest will be counted as income in calculating the taxable amount of your Social Security income. That could increase the amount you owe."

As you can see, there are so many ways to shift and eliminate your tax burden toward the goal of Tax Zero. While no one would confuse municipal bonds with a thrill ride, they are a great strategy to reduce your tax liability. A case could be made for them as one of the top three strategies in this book. However, because they impact Social Security taxes, we list this as number eight.

EPILOGUE

Into the Tax-Zero Future

I tease my mom about buying me a generic Bucket O' Oats and buying the grandkids delicious Honey Bunches of Oats (not to mention buying plenty of extra almonds). But I wrote this book for my parents and others who are planning for what happens as they near retirement age. So many changes happen as you retire, and I want as many people as possible to enjoy financial stability in those years when income changes, but as it turns out, tax liability can increase.

Not today, Devil!

There is no doubt that tax laws will change in the future. I'm glad my team and I saw what was happening with the Tax Cuts and Jobs Act and could help our clients plan and prepare. A lot of these strategies transcend tax code changes, and some will need to be modified to include changes in tax law. I am now hypersensitive to the impact such changes can have as people enter retirement, so my team and I are vigilant and always looking for new strategies.

If you are just retiring, nearing the age when required minimum distributions (RMDs) kick in, this is good information for you to have; it's kind of the sweet spot. But if you are over seventy-two, you can benefit from following many of these strategies. And if you're fifty, it is not too early to be working on these strategies. Contribute to your Roth and max it out. Set money aside into an HSA account.

Don't fall for the myth of spending less in retirement unless you already have a detailed plan to do so. A lot of people end up spending more in retirement.

I want everyone to be able to make these plans and have the money to get out there and live their best lives in retirement without having to worry about a heavy tax burden. I want you to go from tax burden to Tax Zero!

APPENDIX

Recap Of Eight Great Zero-Tax Strategies

Strategy #1: Shift Your Tax Allocation

Focus not on what assets you own but on where you own them. Put them in places that will limit your tax liability.

Strategy #2: Harvest Your Tax Losses

Tax harvesting helps get you toward Tax Zero by selling investments that have lost money and claiming that on your tax return.

Strategy #3: Take Advantage Of Permanent Life Insurance

Build the cash value of your policy to leverage as a loan to yourself. This is a "secondary" strategy to use after limiting your tax liability in other ways.

Strategy #4: Control Taxes With Annuities

The key word here is "control." Annuities give you more control over when they become taxable.

Strategy #5: Give Wisely To Charity

There is not one single way to give to charity. Even without the ability to deduct contributions on your tax return, there are ways to give and still get tax advantages.

Strategy #6: Save With A Healthcare Spending Account

I call this the holy grail of Tax-Zero strategies. There are many ways to eliminate the tax burden on healthcare-related expenses.

Strategy #7: Convert To A Roth IRA

While tax deductions are not available on Roth IRA contributions, the money in a Roth grows tax-free and can be withdrawn tax-free when you follow the withdrawal rules.

Strategy #8: Utilize Tax-Free (Sort Of) Bonds

Municipal bonds can be tax-free at both the state and federal levels. However, there are challenges to be aware of with this strategy.

Acknowledgments

I want to extend my heartfelt gratitude to my clients, whose openness and trust have been the driving force behind this book. Your willingness to share your true concerns about retirement and taxes has been invaluable in shaping the insights shared here. Your real-life experiences have not only influenced my approach to retirement planning but have also deepened my understanding of the challenges many face as they plan for the future. Thank you for allowing me to be a part of your journey and for continuously inspiring me to do better in this field.

I also want to express my deepest thanks to my mother, whose love, wisdom, directness, and countless experiences have shaped the person I am today. The lessons she has instilled in me resonate in my work with clients, enabling me to empathize and relate in ways that make a difference. Mom, thank you for being my first teacher in life and for teaching me the art of listening.

About The Author

Josh Bradley is focused on helping clients work toward their retirement dreams through a well-thought-out financial strategy for retirement income.

Josh's interest in finance and problem-solving, along with his desire to make a positive impact on others' lives, drew him to the financial services industry in 2006. After serving as an independent financial advisor with Voya Financial, he decided to form Capital City Financial Partners in 2016.

As an investment advisor representative, Josh has a fiduciary duty to offer only strategies that are in his clients' best interest. He enjoys helping clients identify their goals and then creating a plan to help them accomplish those goals, and he is committed to earning their trust by providing the highest level of service.

Josh is an investment advisor representative who has passed the Series 66 security exam and holds insurance licenses in South Carolina, North Carolina, Georgia, Florida, Ohio, Tennessee, and Massachusetts.

A lifelong resident of the Columbia, South Carolina, area, Josh attended the University of South Carolina before joining the South Carolina Air National Guard. He and his wife, Ashlie, who also served in the Air Guard, have three daughters and a son. In his spare time, Josh enjoys being with his family, traveling, and cheering on USC sports.

Works Cited And End Notes

1 David C. McKnight, David C. *The Power of Zero: How to Get to the 0 percent Tax Bracket and Transform Your Retirement* (New York, Currency, 2018).

2 Download a copy of the Capital Confidence Plan here: https://capitalcityfinancialpartners.com/book/.

3 Guy Birken, Emily. "Your 'Longevity Literacy' Can Make or Break Your Retirement Planning." *Fast Company,* September 30, 2023. https://www.fastcompany.com/90959041/good-retirement-planning-requires-longevity-literacy.

4 Tax Foundation. "Step-Up in Basis | TaxEDU Glossary." Tax Foundation. February 23, 2024. https://taxfoundation.org/taxedu/glossary/step-up-in-basis/#:~:text=The percent20step percent2Dup percent20in percent20basis,tax percent20owed percent20by percent20the percent20recipient.

5 Bonny, Michael. "5 Businesses Saved by Cash Value Life Insurance." Paradigm Life. January 20, 2024. https://paradigmlife.net/5-businesses-saved-cash-value-life-insurance.

6 Egan, John. "Guide to Annuity Taxes." Forbes Advisor, January 26, 2024. https://www.forbes.com/advisor/retirement/annuity-taxes/.

7 Gleckman, Howard. "21 Million Taxpayers Will Stop Taking Charitable Deductions under the New Tax Law." *Forbes*, January 11, 2018. https://www.forbes.com/sites/beltway/2018/01/11/21-million-taxpayers-will-stop-taking-charitable-deductions-under-the-new-tax-law/?sh=472f0bdc238f.

8 Fíonta, and Fíonta. "Latest Data Shows That the Tax Cuts and Jobs Act Did Not Dampen Charitable Giving." *Tax Foundation*. July 24, 2023. https://taxfoundation.org/blog/tax-cuts-jobs-act-affect-charitable-giving/.

9 Rodeck, David. "How to Make an HSA Part of Your Retirement Plan." *Forbes Advisor*, May 17, 2023. https://www.forbes.com/advisor/retirement/hsa-heath-savings-account-retirement-planning/.

10 O'Connor, Brian J. "January Is Nearly Over. Have You Done Your Retirement Review?" *New York Times*, January 27, 2024. https://www.nytimes.com/2024/01/27/business/retirement-plan-tax-insurance-money-finance.html.

11 SEC.gov. "SEC.gov | What Are Municipal Bonds." www.sec.gov, April 6, 2023. https://www.sec.gov/munied.

12 Tracy, Thom. "Think Twice Before Buying Tax-Free Municipal Bonds." *Investopedia*. February 26, 2024. https://www.investopedia.com/articles/investing-strategy/090116/think-twice-buying-taxfree-municipal-bonds.asp.

Index

Made in the USA
Coppell, TX
16 October 2026

90923141R00059